THE NEW PLANT LIBRARY

CACTI

THE NEW PLANT LIBRARY

CACTI

TERRY HEWITT
Photography by Peter Anderson

AURA

This edition published in 1998 by
Aura Books plc

© Anness Publishing Limited 1998

Produced by
Anness Publishing Limited
Hermes House
88-89 Blackfriars Road
London SE1 8HA

A CIP catalogue record for this book is available from the British Library.

ISBN 1 901683 60 5

Publisher Joanna Lorenz
Editor Margaret Malone
Designer Julie Francis
Photographer Peter Anderson

Printed in Hong Kong

1 3 5 7 9 10 8 6 4 2

Contents

Introduction

*T*o many, a cactus is the tall, spiny plant that they have seen in films of the wild west. There are, in fact, nearly 2,500 different species and an even greater number of distinctive forms. They range from small, button-like plants, less than 2.5cm (1in) across, to barrel-shaped plants and tall, columnar cacti, 9m (30ft) or more high. There are also many leaf-like rain-forest cacti, which are grown for their magnificent flowers.

Cacti are not demanding plants and will tolerate periods of complete neglect, even the dry atmosphere of central heating, and still produce glorious flowers. The purpose of this book is to help you enjoy and care for your plants, so that they can reward you by growing into magnificent specimens, producing lots of beautiful flowers.

■ RIGHT
This prickly pear, *Opuntia lindheimeri* f. *aciculata,* with its dense glochids, is one of the prettiest forms of this species.

The history of cacti

The first cacti were introduced to Europe in the mid-15th century. Christopher Columbus brought back samples of *Melocactus* and *Opuntia* (prickly pear), from the West Indies and presented them to Queen Isabella of Spain.

The most famous of the early herbals was published in 1597 by John Gerard entitled *The Herball or Generall Historie of Plants*. In it, Gerard described four species of "Hedgehogge Thistle", a *Melocactus,* two *Cereus* and an *Opuntia*. In the late 18th century, interest in these unusual plants grew greatly and the number of botanical expeditions became much more frequent. Some of the early species collected were worth more than their weight in gold. The scarcity of these early examples restricted their distribution in cultivation to the nobility, who had large heated orangeries in which to grow them.

In 1788, Captain Arthur Phillip, the founder of Sydney, introduced the *Opuntia* to Australia, to establish

a cochineal dye industry there. The plant is host to the mealy bug beetle, which was harvested, dried and made into the red dye. Because of the very favourable conditions in Australia, the plant soon escaped into the wild and rapidly became a noxious weed, covering large areas of land.

Towards the end of the 19th century, however, interest in cacti waned as orchids became the favourites of the wealthy growers. Despite this, expeditions to collect plants from different parts of the world did not cease, and these led to over 10,000 different cacti species

■ RIGHT
Tall columnar cacti, such as this *Stenocereus thurberi,* have been used as building materials or to make screens and fences by the native inhabitants of the Americas.

■ LEFT AND BELOW
In South America, the soft, long hair-like spines of the *Oreocereus,* (left) have been used to stuff pillows, whilst in Mexico, the stout hooked spines of the *Ferocactus* (below) were used as fish hooks.

These days, conservation is much more in people's minds and efforts are being made to try to preserve the plants in the wild. Growers are encouraged to raise species from seed rather than buy plants that may have been taken from the wild. It is, however, extremely difficult in some of the poorer countries to convince the very needy that their "spiny weeds" are botanically valuable and should be left alone to grow naturally.

In certain parts of the world, governments have set up programmes to help the local people understand the benefits of their native flora, explaining how it can generate income, particularly from tourism.

Cacti have always been used by the local people and are even mentioned in early Aztec writings. There were a multitude of local uses: for example, prickly pears were used to make hedges and barriers to keep stock in and invaders out. Some of the prickly pears have large, tasty fruit and these can still often be found in markets in the warmer countries. In more remote areas, locals still use the dried skeletons of the columnar cacti and chollas as fire wood.

Perhaps the major commercial use of cacti today is to produce cochineal, the natural red dye which is used in the cosmetics industry, particularly as a colourant in lipsticks.

being identified, although the number of different species has recently been reduced to about 2,500, with many varieties and forms. As most of these plants come from fairly hostile terrain, often with a sparse population, many of the areas where cacti are known to occur still have not been botanically explored. Hardly a week goes past without some new species or form being discovered.

Although many plants are now endangered in the wild, often through urbanization, new roads, reservoirs and so on, all cacti have been put on the endangered list and are covered by an international treaty banning their collection in the wild without special permits. International trade is also controlled and the exporter/importer needs to obtain the requisite licences.

What is a cactus?

All over the globe, nature has managed to adapt plants to suit a wide range of unusual environments, from ponds to deserts. In arid areas, plants have had to adapt to receiving only small, irregular amounts of moisture and one of the ways they do this is to store water like a camel until it is needed. The growing conditions they need, therefore, are completely different from the requirements of the plants that we are accustomed to see in our gardens, which have adapted to a regular rainfall.

A brief introduction to cacti will help the reader to understand them better and be able to cope with their requirements which, in turn, will make cultivation much easier. Many problems can be solved using normal gardening techniques, keeping in mind that these plants need less water than normal and object to very low temperatures.

Plants that store moisture are said to be succulent and they can store moisture in one of three ways: in their stems, in their leaves or in their roots. It is almost impossible to draw up an accurate botanical description for this group of plants that excludes other plants such as onions, dahlias, potatoes, and so on. There are also some more woody plants that have adapted to periods of drought, and these are called xerophytes.

Botanical characteristics

Cacti are stem succulents, and whilst it is true that all cacti are succulents, not all succulents are cacti.

To be classified as a cactus, a plant must satisfy four botanical criteria: it must be a perennial; it must be a dicotyledon (possessing a two-leaved embryo); it must produce single-celled fruit; it must have an areole. This last feature is only found in the plant family *Cactaceae*. The areole is a modified axillary bud, from which all growth takes place; side branches, flowers and spines.

Cacti can be split into two main groups; those from desert areas and those from rainforests. The desert cacti have a prime need to conserve moisture and the shape they have adopted, providing them with the smallest surface area and maximum volume, is spherical or globular. Many of the plants are ribbed like a concertina, so that they can expand and contract as moisture becomes available, without splitting their skins. The ribs also help to create a

■ RIGHT
The areole is visible on many cacti as a small, woolly pad at the base of the spines. A modified leaf bud, all growth, including side branches, flowers and spines takes place from it.

■ LEFT
On some of the flat-stemmed rainforest cacti, such as the Christmas cactus shown here, the areole is barely visible in the notches at the side of the leaf-like stem.

■ BELOW

Many features of cacti are designed to minimize water loss; such as their waxy skin and concertina-like ribbing.

■ LEFT

Spines act as important additional dew-points, collecting moisture from fogs, mists and dews occurring at night in desert areas.

microclimate by casting some shade over the rest of the plant.

Some cacti have to compete with other plants, such as grasses and shrubs, and need to reach the light; consequently they become columnar with age. These are the cactus "trees" so often seen in Western films. In the wild, these plants often grow in arid, hostile areas with low rainfall.

Cacti mostly come from rocky and hilly desert areas, rather than sand deserts such as the Sahara. Where these plants grow on the edges of hostile areas, they are probably the last survivors of previous vegetation, rather than colonizers of these areas.

In rainforests, many cacti have developed broad, thin, strap- or leaf-like stems. Here, conservation of

moisture is no longer as important but, where the rainforest is dense, light is the scarcest commodity.

The sharp spines of cacti have many functions. Probably one of the most important is to act as additional dew-points, though they also help to provide a microclimate around the plant, reducing the moisture that can be lost through evaporation. Some cacti are so densely spined that they look as if they are covered in cotton wool. These cacti come from high altitudes, where the spines act as shade in the summer and a cocoon in winter. Although the spines give some protection from animals, many birds nest in them, rodents detach pieces to pull into their burrows, and goats seem oblivious to them.

Many cacti have a very waxy skin, with few pores, to cut down water loss. But this also has an opposite affect: they cannot absorb moisture through their skin.

Cacti are natives of the Americas, with the exception of a few species with very sticky seeds, which are found on migratory bird routes. They can be found just inside Canada (where they are covered in snow in winter to protect them) down to Chile and Argentina, and through the offshore islands. The majority occur in the southern United States, down to northern and central South America. Elsewhere in the world, they have been introduced by man.

■ BELOW

Most cacti are shallow-rooted so that their extensive root system can make use of any night-time precipitation.

Cactus plant groups

Cacti can be broadly divided into four simple groups which serve as a helpful guide when first trying to familiarize yourself with the many different species. The great diversity within nature, however, means that there will always be exceptions to these divisions. Most columnar cacti, for example, are globular when very young and likewise, with great age, many globular cacti can take on the appearance of a columnar cactus.

Rainforest cacti

These plants usually have flattened, leaf-like or cylindrical stems and are often pendant in habit. They are mostly large growing, make ideal subjects for hanging baskets, and are cultivated for their flowers. Not as drought-resistant as the desert plants, they prefer humidity and shade during the brightest parts of the year. Plants such as the Christmas and Easter cacti and the orchid cactus *(Epiphyllum)* belong to this group.

Prickly pears

Opuntias often have flattened, disc-like pads arranged on top of each other like bunnies' ears. These plants are usually collected for their appearance and spination. The spines of many of this group are usually only lightly attached to the plant and are often barbed, which makes them painful to brush against. These plants require very bright conditions.

Rainforest cactus
Selenicereus chrysocardium

Prickly Pear
Opuntia

Columnar cacti

This group contains mostly large-growing plants, ultimately becoming the familiar desert "trees". Many will not flower until they are at least 1.2m (4ft) tall. Larger specimens make good feature plants, both indoors and outside in warm climates, and add height to a collection. They require bright conditions. Comparatively fast-growing, they will respond to good cultivation and the application of suitable fertilisers.

Columnar cactus
Cleistocactus strausii

Globular cacti

This term usually refers to the smaller-growing plants, such as *Parodia, Rebutia, Gymnocalycium, Mammillaria,* which, strictly speaking, are not all globular. This group is usually the most popular with cactus collectors, because many are small-growing and most will flower in a 7.5cm (3in) pot. In a cool climate, some will take years to fill a 13cm (5in) pot. Plants are collected both for their appearance and their attractive flowers. Most require bright conditions.

Globular cactus
Ferocactus herrerae

Growing cacti

Although these plants come from a wide variety of natural conditions, with some basic knowledge, most people will find that cacti are fairly easy and satisfying to grow. In areas which have frost in winter, the plants will need some protection, perhaps in a greenhouse or indoors on a window-sill during the colder months.

■ **BELOW**
Columnar cacti make interesting, unusual features. Highlight the engaging effect by growing them in hand-painted pots.

■ **ABOVE**
Cacti are ideal subjects for a bright, sunny spot in the house, such as a windowsill. Combine with other succulent plants to obtain a wider range of textures, shapes and colours.

Indoor cultivation

Most desert cacti make ideal plants for indoor culture as they come from areas of low humidity. In modern, centrally heated houses, the warmer and drier conditions are often unsuitable for many of the more popular houseplants, making cacti a good alternative.

As cacti are comparatively slow-growing, and many of the globular plants will flower quite easily in 7.5–10cm (3–4in) pots, they are ideal subjects for a bright, sunny window-sill. Plants in the *Mammillaria, Rebutia, Parodia* and *Gymnocalycium* groups are especially suitable. As these are mostly globular plants, the addition of a few taller columnar

cacti, such as *Cereus* or *Cleistocactus,* will enhance the display. The prickly pears are mostly larger-growing plants and are not usually very suitable for indoor spaces, but the small bunny ears of *Opuntia microdasys* is a good choice to add another interesting shape to a collection.

In more humid parts of the house, such as the kitchen or bathroom, a bright position, but out of the full sun, is ideal for rainforest cacti, such as the Christmas cactus (winter-flowering), and orchid cactus (*Epiphyllum*) hybrids.

Some of the larger columnar cacti, for example, prickly pears and barrel cacti, make dramatic feature plants and create a talking point when placed individually or as part of a large group. *Echinocactus grusonii* (golden barrel cactus), the blue column cactus *Cereus hildmannianus* and *Cleistocactus strausii* (silver torch) are always popular for this purpose.

Because cacti are so amenable, they lend themselves to making artistic arrangements, such as cacti gardens, or larger, more permanent displays in beds. Using a variety of

■ ABOVE
Most of the globular cacti make a good place to start building a collection. Appealing both for their shape and flowers, they require only a minimum of effort and many will flower in a 7.5cm (3in) pot.

plants, it is possible to mix shape, colour and texture to create different effects to suit the surroundings. Hunt out a specialist local nursery for a good selection of plants to choose from. Decorate or hand-paint pots and containers to further enhance your display.

■ RIGHT

This alpine carpeting tephrocactus (*Opuntia microsphaericus*) will grow easily outdoors, requiring little attention.

Outdoor cultivation

If you are fortunate enough to live in a mostly frost-free area, cacti can be grown outdoors. The plants require good drainage and, depending on the winter temperatures, protection from the winter rains if in a cool area. Generally, cacti seem able to tolerate temperatures about 2–3°C (2°F) lower when they are growing outdoors, than in a greenhouse, perhaps because of the better airflow around them.

When grown outdoors in beds, many of the smaller-growing plants look lost, except to the experienced eye. Larger-growing plants are much more popular for this reason. The tall columnar cacti, such as *Cereus, Cleistocactus* and *Echinopsis* (*Trichocereus* group) will add height and make a background. Prickly pears will add a more bushy shape with their flat, plate-like pads. Barrel cacti (*Ferocactus* and *Echinocactus*) will add big ball shapes. The spaces between and in front can then be filled with clumping plants, such as *Echinocereus* and *Mammillaria,* which are mainly robust and easy to grow. Small globular shapes can be provided with *Parodia* and *Gymnocalycium.* Some *Rebutia,* although very small-growing, should be included, as these have bright, showy flowers and are usually

■ LEFT

When purchasing cacti, remember that the flowering time is relatively brief. Size and shape can be just as important in creating dramatic arrangements around the garden.

■ LEFT
If planting cacti and
succulents outdoors
in containers, use
terracotta or other
heavy pots which will
not be blown over by
the wind.

the first plants to herald a new season
of activity in the garden. Local
nurseries or garden centres will be
able to advise on plants suitable for
your area.

In colder climates, plants can be
placed outdoors in summer in
containers to decorate and add
interest to the garden. Terracotta or
heavy containers are best for cacti,
because the compost (soil mix) in
them will dry more quickly after rain.

An unusual display can be created
by plunging the pots into beds and
creating a summer cactus garden. A
raised bed, small or large, can be
used, and the size will dictate the
most suitable plants for it. The beds
can be top-dressed with gravel and
stones, to create a more natural-
looking effect.

■ LEFT
The sun-loving
Pilocereus alensis
occurs in northern
South and Central
America and is an
ideal plant for
growing in
warmer areas. The
mature plant
develops a mass of
woolly spines at
the crown.
Nocturnal,
funnel-shaped
flowers grow from
this "beard" from
spring to autumn.

■ BELOW
Specialist nurseries are ideal places for
newer collectors to discover the wonderful
variety that exists among cacti.

Greenhouse cultivation

Perhaps you are lucky enough to have
a greenhouse, or are going to build
one to house your plants? Cacti will
certainly grow better in a greenhouse
than indoors. The greenhouse will
need to be kept frost-free in winter,
preferably with a minimum
temperature of at least 5°C (41°F),
depending on the plants grown.
Good air circulation is a great
advantage and will help to cut down
on damping-off and other problems
in the winter. During the summer,
good ventilation will help to cool the
plants and stop them scorching in the
hottest parts of the year.

With more space available than
indoors, it is possible to grow some of
the larger-growing cacti, such as the
columnar types and prickly pears.
Choosing plants with different shapes
and colours adds much more interest
to the collection. While it is
wonderful when the plants are in
flower, remember that the flowers are
only there for a small part of the year.

Use the extra space that a
greenhouse provides to have a varied
collection of plants. You may find
that, as time progresses, you wish to
concentrate on a smaller group of
plants which you find most

interesting; however, most collectors
find that, over the years, their
interests develop and change.

Most of the plants featured in this
book are comparatively easy to
acquire and grow, and would make
an ideal base for any collection. Some
people prefer the small and more
delicate shapes of *Rebutia* and
Mammillaria, while others like the
rugged shapes of the prickly pears,
barrel cactus and columnar cactus.
Some collect only plants that flower
easily, such as *Rebutia, Mammillaria*
and *Parodia;* others collect only

white-spined plants. Plants from a
small given area or country appeal to
some collectors, but many of these are
rare and often difficult to track down
and acquire.

A good guide for newer collectors
is to collect the plants that genuinely
appeal. At the extreme, thematic
collectors end up growing plants that
fit their theme but that they do not
like particularly or, conversely, they
do not grow plants that they do like
for the same reason! Though
ultimately rewarding, collecting can
have its complications.

■ BELOW
A typical collection of cacti housed in a greenhouse. Most collections are varied in size, shape and colour. The newer additions on the shelf will grow to larger specimens like those in the foreground.

Aporocactus

There are many variables when growing plants, not least the actual vigour of the seedling. In order to give the reader some idea of what they may expect, an average size and spread after five years from seed (or cuttings in a few instances) has been supplied for each plant. These figures are just a guide, however, and with experience and care, you should achieve even better results. Remember also, when grown outdoors in beds, growth rate can be much more rapid, but it does depend on the climate.

Aporocactus are a small group of Mexican epiphytic plants, commonly known as rat's tail cacti and are ideal for hanging baskets. Their attractive red or lilac flowers are produced easily in early spring on all but the smallest plants. The plants are not difficult to grow, needing a minimum temperature a little above freezing. Keeping the plants at 6°C (43°F) will enable the occasional light winter watering to prevent die-back from the tips of the stems. During the warmer months of the year, the plants require a little shade, and need regular watering as soon as they dry out.

■ RIGHT
APOROCACTUS FLAGELLIFORMIS

This is probably the easiest species to grow, with its slender pendant cylindrical stems up to 2m (6ft) or more in length. There is also a red-flowered form (*A. flagriformis*), which is smaller-growing. Five years old pot culture: length 1.5m (5ft); spread 25cm (10in).

Plant Catalogue

Astrophytum

Cephalocereus

A group of four, slow-growing, sun-loving Mexican species, initially globular but becoming columnar in great age. They need extra calcium in the compost (soil mix) for a good root system, otherwise they become difficult to grow. During summer, do not over-water; keep completely dry in winter, or they are prone to rotting. Yellow flowers are produced frequently in summer. Minimum temperature: 6°C (43°F).

■ ABOVE
ASTROPHYTUM MYRIOSTIGMA

These plants are virtually spineless, with four to eight clearly defined ribs. The plant bodies appear grey, because of the numerous small, whitish dots of minute spines. There are many forms, including a spineless form which is dark green. The bright yellow flowers are smaller than the other species in this genus. Five years old pot culture: height 2-5cm(¾–2in); spread 2-2.5cm (¾-1in).

■ BELOW
ASTROPHYTUM ORNATUM

This is perhaps the easiest species to grow and has angular ribs, crowned with clusters of golden straw-coloured spines. The flowers are quite large and bright yellow. There are many different forms of this species. Five years old pot culture: height 5cm (2in); spread 2–2.5 cm (¾–1in).

This small group of tall, slow-growing cacti is usually represented only by *C. senilis* in cultivation.

■ ABOVE
CEPHALOCEREUS SENILIS
(OLD MAN CACTUS)

The long white hair of this attractive species makes it very popular with collectors. The plants may take 50 years to grow 2m (6ft) tall. This species seems to benefit from the addition of calcium to the soil. Plants are prone to rotting if over-watered and should be grown in a well drained compost (soil mix) and allowed to dry out before watering again. Water should be completely withheld from late autumn until early spring. Minimum winter temperature: 7°C (45°F). Full sun. Five years old pot culture: height 7.5 cm (3in); spread 2cm (¾in).

Cereus

Cleistocactus

This large South American group of tall-growing, columnar cacti often make tree-like plants in the wild. Their frequently large, showy flowers (pollinated by moths), are produced at night in order to conserve moisture, the flowers die in the morning as the temperature rises. Easy to grow and relatively quick-growing. Minimum temperature: 6°C (43°F) for most species.

These are slender, South American columnar cacti, sometimes erect, sometimes arching to make colonies. Many have a tubular flower and are pollinated by humming-birds. The tubular flowers hold the nectar, and encourage birds to drink and pollinate the flowers at the same time. Large plants flower from spring to autumn. Minimum winter temperature: 6°C (43°F).

■ ABOVE
CLEISTOCACTUS STRAUSII
(SILVER TORCH)

■ ABOVE
CEREUS HILDMANNIANUS
(SYN C. PERUVIANUS)

This is probably the most commonly grown species and quickly makes large specimen columns, with deeply angled, blue stems. The monstrous (deformed) form shown here is popular for its unusual and irregularly shaped stems. Five years old pot culture: height 25cm (10in); spread 2.5cm (1in).

This is one of the most impressive columnar cacti when fully grown, producing stems up to 3m (10ft) tall, densely covered in shining white spines. The dark tubular flowers are produced in spring. Grow in a reasonably large pot because if the plants are starved, the stems become blind and produce lots of short offsets. Five years old pot culture: height 20cm (8in); spread 2.5cm (1in).

■ ABOVE
CLEISTOCACTUS WINTERI SYN.
BORZICACTUS SAMAIPATANUS;
B. AUREISPINUS

These two species have now been amalgamated into one. Both are spreading or trailing plants, producing red and orange flowers. Easy to grow, they flower when 30–60cm(1–2ft) tall. The flowers open wide at the tips. Five years old pot culture: length 30cm (1ft); spread 2cm (¾in).

Coryphantha

Commonly known as the beehive cactus. Most plants in this group of about 50 small, mostly globular to short cylindrical plants come from Mexico. Most have relatively large, yellow flowers, produced from the crown of the plant in summer. Many species clump freely, to make mounds, but a few remain solitary. Comparatively easy, but slow, to grow, most need to be at least 5 years old from seed to flower. Minimum temperature: 3°C (38°F).

■ ABOVE
CORYPHANTHA CLAVA

This plant grows cylindrical stems, initially erect but becoming prostrate with age. The plants tend to exude a sugary solution when growing. They are best sprayed regularly in summer and autumn. Add a small amount of washing-up liquid to the water, as this helps to wash off the sugar and prevent fungal growth. Five years old pot culture: height 10cm (4in); spread 2.5cm (1in).

■ LEFT
CORYPHANTHA SULCATA

The globular heads on this species clump readily, to make large plants. Attractive and easy to grow. Five years old pot culture: height 5cm (2in); spread 5cm (2in).

Echinocactus

Originating in the United States and Mexico, *Echinocactus* plants are fairly difficult to grow and flower. *E. grusonii* is more closely related to *Ferocactus,* and is certainly the most popular in the group.

■ ABOVE
ECHINOCACTUS GRUSONII

This large golden barrel cactus is very popular as a feature plant, growing to quite massive proportions. It is also comparatively slow-growing. Under normal pot conditions, it often takes about 40 years to grow to 30cm (1ft) diameter and starts to flower when about 40cm (16in) in diameter. Minimum temperature: 10°C (50°F). Five years old pot culture: height 5cm (2in); spread 7.5cm (3in).

Echinocereus

These mostly clumping plants have short, cylindrical stems. Flower buds are produced in spring inside the plant body just above an areole and then burst through the skin in most species. Flowers vary greatly both in size and colour. Minimum temperature: 1°C (34°F), but they tend to mark at this temperature and are better at 7°C (45°F).

■ BELOW
ECHINOCEREUS COCCINEUS
V. NEOMEXICANUS

This small, clumping species has a variety of flower colours, from pink and orange to red and purple. Stem shape and spination vary. Five years old pot culture: height 10cm (4in); spread 7.5cm (3in).

■ BELOW

ECHINOCEREUS REICHENBACHII

This short, squat, pectinate (comb-like), spined plant branches sparingly. The spines take on different hues during the year, giving coloured bands leading to the name "lace cactus". These pectinate-spined *Echinocereus* are more difficult to grow and usually start into growth much later than the green ones. Be very sparing with water early in the growing season. The purple to pink flowers have a dark base, whereas those in the *E. pectinatus* group (rainbow cactus) have pale bases to the petals. Five years old pot culture: height 10cm (4in); spread 2.5cm (1in).

■ ABOVE

ECHINOCEREUS VIRIDIFLORUS

In common with *E. chloranthus*, these are small, clumping plants with short, pectinate spines, sometimes covering the body of the plant. The small flowers are produced in early spring and are shades of yellowish-green to yellowish-brown. Many different forms exist of these species. Five years old pot culture: height 2.5cm (1in); spread 5cm (2in).

■ ABOVE

ECHINOCEREUS PENTALOPHUS

Similar to *E. cinerascens* but the stems are much thinner, like fingers. Again, these are very variable as to spination. The pink-purple flowers have white bases to the petals. Five years old pot culture: height 10cm (4in); spread 15cm (6in).

Echinopsis

This ever-increasing genus now includes *Chamaecereus, Lobivia, Pseudolobivia, Soehrensia* and *Trichocereus*. Some plants will take low temperatures, down to just above freezing; others need a minimum temperature of about 10°C (50°F) or they mark badly in winter. Plants vary in size from small, globular plants to tall, columnar cacti. Easy to grow and fairly free flowering.

■ ABOVE
ECHINOPSIS AUREA

This small-growing, columnar species is fairly densely covered in spines. It produces small, bright yellow flowers during the summer. Minimum temperature: 6°C (43°F). Five years old pot culture: height 5cm (2in); spread 2.5cm (1in).

■ ABOVE
ECHINOPSIS CHAMAECEREUS

The well-known peanut cactus has recently been transferred to this group. The small, finger- (or peanut-) like stems branch rapidly to make fine clumps. It flowers prolifically, producing its bright red flowers in spring and summer. The funnel-shaped blooms last little more than a day. An easy to grow and almost hardy plant, it seems to need moderate amounts of water to grow and flower well. Minimum temperature: 1°C (34°F). Five years old pot culture from a cutting: height 10cm (4in); spread 15cm (6in).

■ LEFT
ECHINOPSIS HYBRID 'GLORIA'

There are hundreds of hybrids in this genus, cultivated for their beautiful flowers. Some have affinities, like this one, with the old *Trichocereus*. Flower colours vary. Some of the hybrids have been named, although there are many just as beautiful un-named ones. Minimum temperature: 4°C (40°F). Five years old pot culture: height 25cm (10in); spread 10cm (4in).

■ BELOW AND RIGHT
ECHINOPSIS SMRZIANA

This is one of the short, columnar and spreading *Trichocereus*. The thick, robust stems produce large 10–25cm (4–10in), white flowers at night on several occasions during the year.

Most of the old columnar *Echinopsis* (*Trichocereus*) produce large, normally white flowers at night on mature plants. Minimum temperature: 3°C (38°F). Five years old pot culture: height 25cm (10in); spread 7.5cm (3in).

Epiphyllum

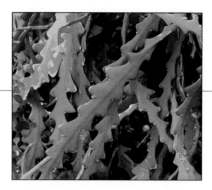

A small group of central American and northern South American rainforest plants, with strap-like stems. Their white flowers are produced at night, mostly with long flower tubes. Flowers are short-lived and, sometimes, scented. Plants require protection from the sun during the hotter months of the year and will benefit from high humidity. Minimum temperature: 10°C (50°F).

■ ABOVE
EPIPHYLLUM ANGULIGER

This is one of the more attractive foliage species, with its "ric-rac" stem. The small, scented flowers are produced in summer. Five years old pot culture from cutting: length 30cm (1ft); spread 15cm (6in).

■ BELOW
EPIPHYLLUM HYBRIDS

The *Epiphyllum* species have been crossed with other genera, such as *Heliocereus, Discocactus* and *Selenicereus,* to produce large, brightly coloured flowers, which are diurnal and last for several days. Most will take a minimum temperature of 6°C (43°F) in winter. Flowers range from white to orange and purple. Flowers vary in size from 10–25cm (4–10in). Five years old pot culture from cutting: height 30–45cm (1–1½ft); spread 10–15cm (4–6in).

Eriosyce

Espostoa

Most of the plants in this recently enlarged genus are better known to collectors as *Neoporteria*. The revision has greatly reduced the confusion caused by plants being classified as *Neochilenia*, *Neoporteria*, *Pyrrhocactus* and *Horridocactus* by different botanists.

Most are easy to grow and many have attractive dark-coloured bodies. Different species flower at different times of the year. Minimum temperature: 7°C (45°F).

These slow-growing, cylindrical, high-altitude South American plants are densely covered in white wool, which acts as protection against the sun in summer and the cold in winter. When the plants are large enough to flower, they produce extra-dense wool down one side of the stem and, from this, the small, creamy white flowers appear. They are night-flowering, foul-smelling and pollinated by bats. Minimum temperature: 7°C (45°F).

■ ABOVE
ERIOSYCE SUBGIBBOSA V. NIGRIHORRIDA

Much better known under its old name, *neoporteria,* this globular plant eventually becomes columnar. Its dark spines, dark body and bright red flowers make it a desirable plant to grow. Five years old pot culture: height 7.5cm (3in); spread 2.5cm (1in).

■ LEFT
ERIOSYCE SENILIS (NEOPORTERIA VILLOSA F. LANICEPS)

This small, hairy species becomes shortly columnar in age. The attractive flowers are produced in spring and autumn. Five years old pot culture: height 7.5cm (3in); spread 2.5cm (1in).

■ ABOVE
ESPOSTOA LANATA

This species has more slender, taller stems and less wool than many species in the genus. It is comparatively quick to grow and is perhaps the easiest species. Five years old pot culture: height 10cm (4in); spread 2.5cm (1in).

Ferocactus

Commonly referred to as barrel cactus. These large cacti from the southern United States and Mexico make impressive plants with age, some eventually reaching up to 3m (10ft) tall. In cultivation, these plants soon make good specimen plants, although most will not flower until they are at least 25cm (10in) in diameter. Grown for their shape and often fascinating, if fierce, spines.

■ ABOVE
FEROCACTUS GLAUCESCENS

This blue-bodied species has short, straight, golden spines and is easy to grow, although it usually only flowers when it is about 15cm (6in), at least, in diameter. Seems to need a minimum temperature of 7°C (45°F) in winter or the body marks badly. Five years old pot culture: height 7.5cm (3in); spread 7.5cm (3in).

■ LEFT
FEROCACTUS HERRERAE

This large-growing species has fierce, broad, fish-hook-like spines. Grown from seed, these plants can almost appear columnar until the main stem swells to take on a more globular shape. Needs to be about 30cm (1ft) in diameter to flower. Minimum temperature: 6°C (43°F) in winter. Five years old pot culture: height 10cm (4in); spread 2.5cm (1in).

Gymnocalycium

A group of about 80 species and forms of generally small-growing, disc-like to globular plants, mostly from Argentina. Flowers are produced from the crown of the plant during the summer and need bright conditions. Most of the disc-like species are fairly tolerant of cold and need a temperature of at least 3°F (38°C) in winter but the larger globular species, such as *G. saglionis*, need a minimum of 7°C (45°F).

■ BELOW
GYMNOCALYCIUM BRUCHII

This small-headed species has pale pink flowers. Sometimes it is sold as blue-flowered, apparently owing to a printing error in a popular cactus book. Slow-growing, it will form a dense carpet of stems. Five years old pot culture: height 2cm (¾in); spread 7.5cm (3in).

■ ABOVE AND ABOVE TOP
GYMNOCALYCIUM
BALDIANUM

This is one of the more popular, small, disc-like species, as it produces bright red flowers. Five years old pot culture: height 2cm (¾in); spread 5cm (2in).

Mammillaria

Common names include pincushion and nipple cactus. This is one of the largest and most popular of all the globular cacti. They are mostly easy to grow and flower, producing their rings of bright flowers around the crown of the plants in the spring, with a second, and sometimes a third, flush of blooms later on. If the flowers are pollinated, these will produce sausage-shaped fruits (usually bright red) up to a year later. Minimum temperature: 6°C (43°F).

■ ABOVE
MAMMILLARIA HAHNIANA
(OLD LADY CACTUS,
BIRTHDAY CAKE CACTUS)

An old favourite. The globular plants are densely covered in long, curly, hair-like white spines, which can be short or, on some plants, up to 5cm (2in) long, which wrap themselves around the body of the plant. The rings of bright red flowers are followed by rings of even brighter red, small, candle-like seed-pods. Easy to grow, flowering at about 5cm (2in) in diameter. Five years old pot culture: height 5cm (2in); spread 7.5cm (3in).

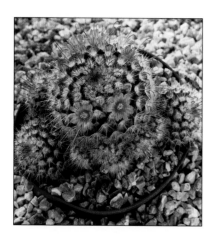

■ ABOVE
MAMMILLARIA BOMBYCINA

There are many forms of this species with spine colours that can be red, brown or yellow. Most clump and make mounds or clusters of thick, short, column-like stems. Some plants can be shy of producing their dainty rings of pink flowers when small. Five years old pot culture: height 7.5cm (3in); spread 7.5cm (3in).

■ ABOVE
MAMMILLARIA BOCASANA

This hemispherical species offsets freely, to make large mounds, producing its mostly cream flowers through a large part of the spring and summer. The dense, white, hairy spines that cover the plant, and fine-hooked red central spines, make this a distinctive plant. Five years old pot culture: height 5cm (2in); spread 10cm (4in).

■ BELOW

MAMMILLARIA MAGNIMAMMA

Many similar species have been amalgamated into this group. They tend to be larger, with globular to flattened bodies, eventually clumping to make large mounds. The plants have large, green tubercles and comparatively few spines, leaving the body clearly visible. The rings of cream, pink or red flowers are mostly smallish, produced in late spring. Easy to grow. Five years old pot culture: height 7.5cm (3in); spread 7.5cm (3in).

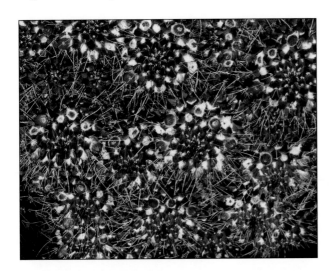

■ ABOVE

MAMMILLARIA PROLIFERA
(STRAWBERRY CACTUS)

This dense, clumping species is easy to grow and was an early introduction to cultivation. The small, yellowish flowers are produced in profusion throughout the spring and summer, followed by short, fat, sausage-like fruit that taste like strawberries. Five years old pot culture: height 2.5cm (1in); spread 10cm (4in).

■ ABOVE

MAMMILLARIA MICROHELIA

The short, fat, finger-like stems are densely covered in spines, usually with a darker central spine. The rings of cream or pink flowers are produced on small plants in early spring. Five years old pot culture: height 7.5cm (3in); spread 2cm (¾in).

■ LEFT

MAMMILLARIA
RHODANTHA

This is one of the larger-growing *Mammillarias*. It makes a short, fat column which, when larger, will branch dichotomously (the growing point elongates and divides), eventually making a large, sprawling clump. Spine colours vary, from brown to golden, all of which are attractive. Although spring-flowering, it will often flower again towards autumn. Five years old pot culture: height 10cm (4in); spread 5cm (2in).

Opuntia

Common names include prickly pear, cholla and bunnies' ears. One of the two largest groups of cacti, it is widespread in the wild from Canada to southern South America. Sizes range from short, ground-covering alpine plants to large tropical trees or bushes covering many acres. Most of the more common species are easy and quick to grow, often outgrowing their allotted space.

They are grown for their attractive shape, as only large specimens will flower. Beware of the spines.

■ ABOVE
OPUNTIA VESTITA

This slender, cylindrical species is covered in long, wool-like spines. It has bright red flowers when the stems are about 30cm (1ft) tall. It is often seen as a crested (cristate) form, with fan-shaped stems. Minimum temperature: 6°C (43°F). Five years old pot culture: height 20cm (8in); spread 7.5cm (3in).

■ ABOVE
OPUNTIA MICRODASYS

Probably the most popular small-growing species. The small pads are spineless although they are neatly arranged with numerous areoles and glochids, which are detached easily if brushed against. There are a variety of spine colours, from white to yellow, brown and reddish. Plants need to be mature to produce their small flowers. Minimum temperature: 10°F (50°C). Five years old pot culture: height 15cm (6in); spread 10cm (4in).

■ LEFT
OPUNTIA LINDHEIMERI
F. ACICULATA

This popular variable species from the United States and Mexico can have few or many spines. The form shown is probably the most attractive. Minimum temperature: 7°C (45°F). Five years old pot culture from a cutting: height 30cm (1ft); spread 15cm (6in).

Oreocereus

Commonly known as old man of the Andes, these plants are well distributed in the Andes and are extremely variable. There have been a large number of different "species" but most are little more than forms of *O. celsianus*. Although in the wild these plants tolerate low temperatures, in cultivation, with our much more humid atmosphere, they seem prone to rotting below 6°C (43°F). Plants are slow-growing, and require careful summer watering and a dry winter.

■ ABOVE

OREOCEREUS CELSIANUS

Probably the most common species, it is variable, giving rise to many different names. The plants have sturdy columns, with various amounts of wool-like spines masking the thick straight ones. They make very attractive plants at any size. Five years old pot culture: height 7.5cm (3in); spread 2.5cm (1in).

■ LEFT

OREOCEREUS TROLLII

Differs from *O. celsianus* in its tight, cocoon-like covering of white spines. The plant needs full sun to thrive. Five years old pot culture: height 7.5cm (3in); spread 2.5cm (1in).

Pachycereus

Parodia

This group of mostly Mexican, columnar cacti make fine, impressive feature plants. Although many are slow-growing, they add a variety of shapes and forms to a plant collection. Minimum winter temperature: 5–15°C (42–60°F), depending on the species.

■ BELOW
PACHYCEREUS PRINGLEI

One of the large, tall-growing cactus often seen in Western films. Although it will grow to massive proportions, it is comparatively slow in cultivation, taking perhaps 10 years to grow 45cm (1½ft) tall. Minimum temperature: 7°C (45°F). Five years old pot culture: height 10cm (4in); spread 2.5cm (1in).

■ ABOVE
PARODIA LENINGHAUSII

The densely spined, golden columns make this a distinctive plant. Although solitary at first, it will, as it gets larger, produce many offsets from the base. The large, yellow flowers are produced on plants taller than about 15 cm (6in). Minimum temperature: 5°C (42°F). Five years old pot culture: height 10cm (4in); spread 5cm (2in).

■ RIGHT
PARODIA MAGNIFICA

This old *Notocactus* deserves its name, as it makes beautiful, large clumps of bluish-green bodies with golden to white spines. Easy to grow. Minimum temperature: 10°C (50°F). Five years old pot culture: height 7.5cm (3in); spread 7.5cm (3in).

This group has recently been expanded to include the former genus *Notocactus.* There were a vast number of species in the old *Parodia* genus and many of these have now been amalgamated as the differences between them were minor.

This group does best given a minimum winter temperature of 10°C (50°F). If the plants are kept completely dry for long periods, they tend to lose their roots and are difficult to re-establish. Growing them at a slightly higher temperature will enable you to give them an occasional small amount of water in good weather in winter.

Rebutia

This genus now includes *Aylostera, Digitorebutia, Rebutia, Sulcorebutia* and *Weingartia*. An attractive, small-growing group of South American cacti, it is one of the first to flower in the spring; the old *Rebutia* group flowers earlier than the *Sulcorebutias,* followed by the *Weingartias*. Most are easy to grow and are able to tolerate temperatures down to near freezing in winter, if kept completely dry.

■ ABOVE
REBUTIA CANIGUERALII
F. RAUSCHII
(SYN. SULCOREBUTIA RAUSCHII)

There are several forms of this plant, many with a deep purple flower. All grow well when grafted, but the green-body form grows more easily on its own roots than the purple form. Five years old pot culture: height 2cm (¾in); spread 5cm (2in).

■ ABOVE
REBUTIA HELIOSA
V. CONDORENSIS

The small, globular heads of this plant are densely covered in short spines, giving it a silvery appearance. It is not an easy plant to grow on its own roots but, grafted, it will make a large and very attractive specimen, producing numerous orange flowers in late spring.

This darker-bodied form, with a less dense covering of spines, has red flowers. Unlike the species, it is easy to grow on its own roots and makes fine clumps. Five years old pot culture: height 2cm (¾in); spread 5cm (2in).

■ LEFT
REBUTIA ARENACEA (SYN. SULCOREBUTIA ARENACEA)

One of the choice *Sulcorebutias*, with its small body, numerous areoles and short spines. The yellow flowers are produced in late spring. Five years old pot culture: height 2cm (¾in); spread 5cm (2in).

■ ABOVE

REBUTIA MARSONERI

This used to be one of the few yellow-flowered *Rebutias* but, now that the genera have been amalgamated, there are many. Easy to grow. Five years old pot culture: height 2.5cm (1in); spread 7.5cm (3in).

■ LEFT

REBUTIA MINUSCULA
F. SENILIS
(SYN. REBUTIA SENILIS)

The squat, green body of this species offsets slowly, to make clumps. The bright red flowers are produced from around the base of the plant. An easy plant to grow, the form shown here is similar to the species but has longer, white, hairy spines and brighter red flowers. Five years old pot culture: height 2.5cm (1in); spread 5cm (2in).

■ BELOW

REBUTIA MUSCULA

This small-headed species clumps easily, to make mounds of dense white heads. Produces its beautiful orange flowers in late spring. Five years old pot culture: height 5cm (2in); spread 7.5cm (3in).

■ ABOVE

REBUTIA MENTOSA (SYN. SULCOREBUTIA
MENTOSA)

This is one of the larger headed *Sulcorebutia* species, normally offsetting when the main head is 5–7cm (2–3in) in diameter. Five years old pot culture: height 2cm (¾in); spread 2.5cm (1in).

Thelocactus

This small group of primarily Mexican plants are mostly flattened discs. Long-lasting flowers are produced from the crown of the plant at intervals in the spring and summer. Do not over-water as they are prone to rot. Minimum temperature: 6°C (43°F).

■ ABOVE

THELOCACTUS BICOLOR

This often pyramidal species comes from the southern United States, where it is known as glory of Texas. Its bright red flowers are perhaps more characteristic of *Echinocactus* than *Thelocactus*. Five years old pot culture: height 5cm (2in); spread 2.5cm (1in).

■ ABOVE
THELOCACTUS
HEXAEDROPHORUS V. LLOYDI

This small, blue to slate-coloured plant is slow-growing and looks rather stone-like, pressed tightly to the ground. The relatively large flowers are produced in spring and summer. Five years old pot culture: height 2cm (¾in); spread 5cm (2in).

■ LEFT
THELOCACTUS
SETISPINUS

This species has been included in many genera but currently rests here. It flowers freely during the summer; its large yellow flowers have a red centre, and are often sweetly scented. It is quite prone to rotting if over-watered and needs about 10°C (50°F) in winter to grow well. Five years old pot culture: height 5cm (2in); spread 5cm (2in).

The Grower's Guide

Choosing and buying cacti

Cacti can easily be purchased from a variety of sources, such as florists, supermarkets and garden centres. Sometimes, though, through the seller's lack of knowledge, the plants are not in very good condition, unless they have been delivered only recently. Often, the plants people see in these outlets do little to encourage new collectors.

Cacti that are well presented show that the grower cares about the plants and has made an effort to get them to the purchaser in good condition. Ideally, plants should be named correctly, but labels do fall out and people reading them put them back in the wrong place, so this is not always the seller's fault.

It is a good idea to buy plants direct from the grower. Many cactus nurseries are open to the public and you will normally get a much wider choice of size and variety than from a retail outlet; you can also judge the overall condition of the plants.

If you are at all doubtful about a plant you have purchased, it is a good idea to repot it. Examine and treat the plant for any pests, and examine the root system; that way, you have a good idea of the plant's condition.

Plants sometimes turn up in unlikely places and, by keeping a look out at church bazaars, school fetes, jumble (tag) sales, car boot (garage) sales and so on, it is often possible to pick up some surprising bargains.

■ ABOVE

Plants should look in good condition and "glow" with health (above left); they should not look tired and miserable. When buying, watch out for plants that are dehydrated, poorly potted and half out of their pots (centre); covered in insect pests (particularly mealy bug), or badly marked (above right).

Care and cultivation

■ BELOW
Compost (soil mix), should contain about one-third grit, with the rest being made up of peat, loam plus a good base fertilizer.

Whether the plants are indoors or out, their requirements are much the same. They require an open, free-draining compost (soil mix), complete with a good base fertilizer.

Cacti are hungry plants and many come from areas which, although low in humus, are rich in mineral content. For the best results, feed the plants regularly, about once a week during the growing season (generally spring until autumn), with a cactus food, or one recommended for tomatoes used at about half strength.

Small plants will soon outgrow their pots and will benefit from being repotted into a larger container. Full-depth pots up to 7.5cm (3in) in depth and diameter are ideal. With wider containers, 10cm (4in) diameter and upwards, use shallower pots, with a depth of only 8–10cm (3–4in) for globular plants. For tall-growing species, however, full-depth pots are more suitable. Ideally, plants should be repotted at least every two years, to freshen the soil and remove build-up of insoluble mineral salts.

Desert cacti

Most of the desert cacti need a bright situation; the larger-growing species need full sun but some of the smaller ones may benefit from slight shading during the height of summer. Good ventilation is essential, but avoid cold draughts.

Like most plants, they will grow when the temperatures are between a certain minimum and maximum. In winter, in a greenhouse in northern Europe, for example, temperatures are usually too low for growth, so the plants have a forced period of dormancy. The other problem is that light levels are also too low for sturdy growth. Growth made during the winter is often misshapen and distorted, and this "soft" growth is much more prone to disease and over-watering. In a greenhouse with a

■ ABOVE
When the weather is warm, water early in the morning or late in the day. Watering from above will also wash the plants clean and remove any dusty deposits.

■ LEFT
In warmer and brighter climates, whilst most desert cacti need full sun, provide the smaller ones with slight shading.

the temperatures, do not flood the plants. Over-watering in mid-summer causes root rot, which often does not show up until the cooler days of autumn, when the plants will dramatically collapse.

Rainforest cacti

These plants generally have flattened, leaf-like stems, and prefer warm and humid conditions for the best growth. Many require a minimum temperature of 10°C (50°F), particularly in winter, and an occasional watering during bright and mild weather. In northern Europe and the northern United States, with normally low winter light levels, plants will benefit from a bright situation. During the rest of the year, rainforest cacti will require some shade from the sun.

These plants need more water than the desert species and will normally grow throughout most of the year, if it is warm enough. In warm weather, water the plants liberally and then wait until they are almost dry before watering again. Winter growth will be weak, due to the lack of light, so just give enough to stop the plants shrivelling and keep them growing slowly.

■ ABOVE
Take care not to over-water cacti during winter; give just enough water to stop too much shrivelling, rather than attempt to encourage growth.

minimum temperature of 6°C (43°F), plants will probably be best left dry from late autumn until early spring, depending upon the weather. On a windowsill in a centrally heated living room, they may need a very small amount of water every couple of weeks during winter.

At the other end of the scale, when temperatures are very high in mid-summer, cacti go into their natural dormant period, to conserve moisture. In the United Kingdom and much of the United States, this is usually from about July until mid-August. During this time, despite

Planting cacti

Growing several plants together in one container is a good way of making an attractive display with a few plants. When choosing a suitable container, keep in mind that the plants need a bright situation. Make sure the container is not too large or the wrong shape for its intended position. Containers can be plastic, terracotta or ceramic, depending on personal choice. A container with drainage holes is easier to look after. Some of the larger bonsai bowls can be used to good effect.

Cactus bowl gardens

The object of a cactus garden is to make a semi-permanent feature or living decoration, so do not encourage rapid growth or one or two plants will soon outgrow the others. During the summer, a regular watering every three to four weeks should be sufficient. Containers without drainage holes need to be watered with caution, so as not to build up a reservoir at their base. Ideally, enough water should be given at a time so that the compost (soil mix) will dry out in about 10 days. The amount will depend on the shape and size of the container, its position and the weather. Feed occasionally, to keep the plants healthy but not in such large quantities that the plants grow too quickly.

When it is finished, stand back and look at the bowl garden. If any changes need to be made, make them now. When it is ready, water lightly overhead with a rose or spray, to settle the gravel and wash the stones clean.

PLANTING A CACTUS BOWL GARDEN

1 Select the plants that you intend to use. Plants that require similar conditions are best grown together. For example, most desert plants are compatible and most rainforest plants will grow together but not the two groups mixed together. Separate the winter-growing Christmas cactus and the summer-growing desert cactus.

2 Stand the container in its eventual home and then place the plants you intend to use in it. Arrange them for the best effect. Do not overcrowd the plants. Putting too many in the same container will detract from its overall appearance and it will soon look overgrown. Arrange for shape, style and colour.

3 Fill the container with a gritty compost (soil mix), carefully plant the specimens and firm the compost (soil mix) well (it is surprising how much it will settle). Decorate the top of the container with some pieces of rock and then top-dress with small gravel. A paint brush is useful for pushing the gravel under the plants.

Raised beds

If you are fortunate enough to live in a frost-free area, cacti can be grown outdoors. The plants need a very well drained soil and this can be achieved by mixing about equal proportions of compost (soil mix) and grit. Raising the bed above ground level makes it easier for the surplus water to drain away. If there is a high rainfall, particularly in winter, the plants will need some form of protection. For those who are not so fortunate, it is also quite easy to construct a bed in a greenhouse or conservatory.

The bed needs a depth of 10–30cm (4–12in) of compost (soil mix), depending on the size of plants to be grown. Permanent beds can be built with brick or stone sides to the desired height. Line the bottom and any exterior walls with polystyrene, to stop the cold from penetrating the bed and affecting the plants. Fill to within 10–30cm (4–12in) of the top with rubble and then cover with a layer of carpet, underfelt or even newspaper, to prevent the compost (soil mix) from sinking into the rubble. Top up the bed with a good, gritty compost (soil mix) containing at least one-third gravel and then firm the bed well, to reduce the degree of subsequent settlement.

A natural type of stone usually enhances the overall appearance; coloured gravels usually detract from it. A light overhead watering will wash the gravel clean, but it is best to allow the compost (soil mix) to settle for a week or so before watering properly.

PLANTING A RAISED BED

1 Arrange the plants on the bed to best effect, allowing sufficient space for them to grow.

2 De-pot the plants and loosen the root ball before planting. Pieces of rock placed between the plants will create a natural-looking effect.

3 When they are all planted, top-dress with gravel. Rake over the surface to level it.

Hanging baskets

Although there are a few desert cacti that have long trailing stems, most are not really suitable for growing in hanging baskets. On the other hand most rainforest cacti are ideally suited to this particular planting method. Many of these plants naturally grow in trees and have pendant branches, such as the epiphytic rainforest cacti which use other plants for support, though they do not actually take any nourishment from them. These rainforest cacti will need some protection from the direct sun in summer. A humid environ ment is ideal for them, and they should be watered well and then allowed to become just dry before watering again. Beware of over-watering very large containers because they can be very slow to dry in cool weather. If space is at a premium, several different species can be planted in the same container – although one or two are sure to outgrow the others. Planting a few smaller plants of the same species in a basket will make a more natural-looking display.

Epiphyllum hybrid

PLANTING A HANGING BASKET

1 Select a basket to suit its location. A wide choice of plastic and wire ones are readily available from gardening outlets. Wire baskets will need to be lined first with sphagnum moss.

2 Fill the basket with compost (soil mix) and arrange the plants so that they are not obstructed by the chains. Make holes and arrange the plants, leaning them outwards to encourage pendant growth.

3 When they are all planted, firm the compost (soil mix) well and top up or remove any surplus so that there is a 2cm (¾in) gap at the top of the basket, to allow for watering.

Routine maintenance

Cacti are, fortunately, fairly undemanding plants and many will survive even after a tremendous amount of neglect. However, it does not require much effort to look after cacti properly and the results will be much more rewarding. For best results, check plants once or twice a month, and when necessary, clean off the dust or tidy up the foliage.

Handling

Many cacti are spiny plants and there are numerous methods for handling them. A pair of domestic rubber gloves gives fairly good protection for smaller plants. Some people prefer to make a paper spill and wrap it around the plant as they are working on it. With larger specimens, often one or two cloths give good protection. Do not use a cloth on hooked-spined plants as it is very difficult to remove the cloth afterwards.

Pruning

This is not usually a problem with cacti, except with old plants that have become very overgrown or tall plants that have become too large.

DUSTING

If you are growing cacti indoors, they tend to accumulate dust. Remove this with a small brush, blow it off with a hair-dryer or wash it off with a spray of water. In a greenhouse, overhead watering will normally remove any build-up of dust.

HANDLING

The most difficult plants to handle are the *Opuntias* (prickly pear) as the barbed spines and numerous sharp glochids are only lightly attached to the plant. A piece of thick foam or polystyrene provides good protection and can be thrown away afterwards.

DAMAGED PLANTS

Epiphytic rainforest cacti, with their leaf-like stems, will occasionally suffer from drought or cold or some other mishap and the thin stems become damaged. These can be removed with a pair of secateurs (pruners) or scissors, to tidy up the plant.

Many of the rainforest cacti – particularly the hybrid *Epiphyllums* – will benefit from the removal of the oldest and often faded growth every few years. With the *Epiphyllum* hybrids, next year's flowers are normally produced on this year's ripened stems. Pruning out the oldest and often discoloured of these stems from time to time will help to keep the plant more compact and manageable.

Globular cacti tend not to mark as rainforest cacti do. Slight damage is not unusual and is probably best left alone, unless unsightly. Some argue that it adds character! Cut out severe damage with a sharp knife.

When tall-growing columnar cacti run out of room to grow any further, it is time to think about cutting them back and starting again. The top piece can be re-rooted and the bottom will normally make several new shoots.

Watering and feeding

Like all plants, cacti must have food, water, light and air to grow. During the spring to autumn period, most should be watered well and then left to dry out before watering again. Weather, situation, compost (soil mix), temperature, pot size and type of plant will all affect how quickly or slowly this happens. Ideally, with larger containers, sufficient water should be given at a time so that the container will dry out again in 10 days. Smaller pots may dry out in two to three days. Growing all your plants in a similar compost (soil mix) makes it easier to judge how often to water. Cacti are quite hungry plants and need to be given a regular dose of food.

PRUNING

When pruning *Epiphyllum* hybrids, first remove any badly damaged or discoloured stems. Next, remove any weak branches growing from towards the tips of the flattened stems. Cut out stems that are crossing over to leave an upright plant.

Cut out any stems that unbalance the plant and any short ones that have not fully developed. Although the plant may be considerably smaller, new growth should now be produced from the base to make a neat and compact shape.

Cut the main stem of a tall columnar cactus with a sharp knife or saw to a suitable length; about half the height you want the plant to be is a good guide, to allow for growth. The base will normally offset from around the cut surface.

Repotting

Cacti should look comfortable in their pots. With most of the small, globular plants, it is time to repot when the plant has almost reached the sides of the pot. It should be repotted into a large enough new pot to leave a 1–2cm (½–¾in) space between the plant and the side of the pot. Larger plants require a little more space, perhaps allowing 2.5–5cm (1–2in) between the plant and the edge of the pot. The best guide really is visual: does the plant look right in the pot? Tall-growing plants should be repotted into a pot in proportion to their height. If the plant is top-heavy or unstable, the pot is certainly too small. A plant 60cm (2ft) tall will need at least a 13cm (5in) pot, and possibly larger. A 1.5m (5ft) tall plant will need at least a 30cm (1ft) pot, both for stability and to allow room for it to grow.

Equipment

To repot a cactus, first assemble all the equipment you will need: a new pot of the right size, enough semi-dry compost (soil mix) to fill the new container and something to hold the plant. A spill of paper is ideal for hooked-spined plants; a piece of cloth, such as an old towel, is ideal for straight-spined plants. Hold large and very fiercely spined plants with a thick piece of foam, plastic or polystyrene. When removing the plant from the pot, if the pot sticks to the roots, a few thumps on a plastic pot will normally free it. The hole in the bottom of clay pots can be used to push plants out through the top of the pot; if not, loosen the soil from the inside of the pot with a knife.

REPOTTING CACTI

1 Hold the plant firmly, gently tip to a horizontal position and slip off the old pot. Keeping the plant in this position, loosen up the root ball and remove as much of the old compost (soil mix) as possible.

2 Try positioning the plant in its new container. See how much compost (soil mix) is required under the plant so that the gap between soil level and the rim of the pot is as before.

3 Fill the container to within about 0.5–1cm (¼–½in) of the top and top-dress with gravel, if desired. Do not water for several days, to allow any damaged roots to grow calluses.

It is particularly important to remove the old compost (soil mix) from the plant when repotting. This is especially true if using a different type of compost (soil mix); that is, if you are changing from or to a peat-based compost (soil mix) or soil-based one, as there is often little interchange of moisture between the different types of composts (soil mix).

Sometimes, with a very spiny plant or a delicate one, repotting can be made easier by placing a pot the same size as the current one inside the new larger pot, as shown below.

After a plant has been in a pot for two or three years, the compost (soil mix) will have become compacted and both air and water will have difficulty getting to the roots. In hard-water areas, the level of chalk (lime) will also have increased, together with any unused compounds from feeding. Most cacti will, therefore, benefit from repotting from time to time, even if only to freshen the compost (soil mix). Ideally, repot small plants every two to three years, and large ones every three to five years.

■ ABOVE
Cacti should be in proportion to their pots. Smaller plants need approximately 1-2cm (½–¾in) in space between the plant and the side of the pot, larger plants require more space, up to 2.5-5cm (1-2in).

REPOTTING SPINY OR DELICATE CACTI

1 Put an empty pot that is the same size as the one the plant is currently in, into the centre of the new, larger container. Fill the space between the two pots with compost (soil mix) and then firm well.

2 Carefully remove the empty, inner pot. Ease out the plant and gently break up the bottom 1cm (⅜in) of old compost (soil mix), then carefully drop the plant into the hole in the new container.

3 With a dibber or stick, gently firm the compost (soil mix) around the plant. This method is particularly useful for larger, hooked-spined plants.

Propagation

Cacti are, mostly, easy plants to propagate, whether by cuttings, from seed or by grafting. Each method has its place and, with a little practice, can be used to increase the size of any plant collection. There is great satisfaction in turning a seed or cutting into a beautiful plant.

When cacti are mature, they will flower. Many species will do this when less than 7.5cm (3in) in diameter. There are, however, many tall-growing species, which need to be larger to flower – 90cm (3ft) or more.

The flower contains all the parts necessary for the plants to produce seed. Some cacti are self-fertile;

that is, they can be fertilized with their own pollen: many others, however, need pollen from another plant to complete the process. Seeds develop in the ovary, which swells and ripens before the seed can be harvested to grow more plants.

When the pods are ripe and soft, open them and spread the often sticky contents on paper to dry. Wash very sticky seeds in warm water. When the seeds are dry, either store or sow them, depending on the time of year and facilities available. Many cactus seeds will be viable for many years but, for most, it will decline after the first one or two years.

■ ABOVE
The stigma, the female receptive organ, is in the centre of the flower; the stamens carrying the pollen (male part) surround the stigma, and the ovary, the chamber where the seeds develop, is at the base of the stigma.

PROPAGATION BY SEED

1 In order to set seed the flower must be pollinated. Transfer pollen from the stamens to the stigma using a small, clean paintbrush. Some cacti are self-fertile, others need another plant of the same species in flower.

2 After pollination the flower withers and the ovary develops into a fruit containing seed. It can take many months before it ripens and softens or splits open.

3 Ripe seed pods can be split open and the contents spread on to paper to dry. Seed can be sown immediately or stored when dry.

Growing from cuttings

Growing from cuttings is an easy way to increase the variety of a collection.

Cactus cuttings can be from 5cm (2in) to 2m (6ft) long, depending on the plant. After you have taken cuttings, allow them to dry and the cut surface to become callused. This can be a week, or less in summer for small cuttings. During the winter it can take two to three months, or longer for larger cuttings. The ideal time for taking cuttings is late spring to mid-summer, so that the cuttings will have as much time as possible to establish in the warmer weather, before the cold and damp of winter.

Small cuttings are easily rooted in a seed tray. Place the tray in a warm, bright and airy place; a gentle bottom heat of about 24°C (75°F) should speed up the rooting process. The compost (soil mix) should be kept just slightly damp. When there are signs of active new growth, pot up the rooted cuttings individually. They will start to root in one to six weeks.

Tall cuttings will not stand up in a shallow container. Take a pot as small as possible, in which the cutting will stand up. Quarter-fill the pot with compost (soil mix) and cover with a layer of fine gravel. Stand the cutting on the gravel and fill the pot with more gravel. The weight of the gravel should keep the cutting upright. The collar of stones around the plant will help to prevent rotting, while the humidity of the compost (soil mix) will encourage it to root. Large cuttings may take six months to root.

When new growth can be seen at the top of the stem, lay the pot on its side and carefully tip out the gravel. The compost (soil mix) at the bottom should be full of roots. Stand the pot upright, fill with compost (soil mix) and allow the plant to make a good root system. After three to six months, repot into a larger container.

PROPAGATION BY CUTTINGS

1 Tall, columnar cacti often have a woody vascular bundle and a sharp saw or knife can be used to cut through this. For smaller cuttings, a scalpel or small, sharp knife is ideal.

2 Small cuttings can easily be rooted in a seed tray. Fill with compost (soil mix) to within 1cm (½in) of the top and very gently firm. Fill the tray to the top with 1cm (½in) of fine grit.

3 Gently push the cuttings into the grit, just deep enough for them to stand up. This will keep the damp compost (soil mix) away from the base of the cutting.

Growing from seed

Seed is best sown in a heated propagator in late winter, so the seedlings have the maximum time to grow as large as possible before the following winter. If you do not have a propagator, wait until the weather warms up in late spring or early summer before sowing.

Fifty seeds can be sown in a 7.5cm (3in) pot or 1,000 in a standard seed tray. Individual pots are better, to allow for the differing germination rates of various species.

When the seeds have germinated, they will grow well under normal greenhouse conditions with a minimum temperature of 10°C (50°F). The seedlings should be protected from direct, strong sunlight. Young cactus seedlings, little bigger than the head of a match, spend their first one to three months developing a root system. Until the roots have developed sufficiently, there is hardly any growth in the plant body. By about three months, the seedlings are starting to grow and will continue to develop while the

growing conditions are favourable. They should now be treated like slightly more delicate adult plants.

Cactus seedlings have delicate, fine roots which are easily damaged. It is much better to leave the germinated seedlings alone for as long as possible unless some problem necessitates treatment. So long as they are not too dense, they can be left alone for as long as two years.

When they have grown to a manageable size, prick out the seedlings. Cacti seedlings are never uniform in their growth rate and

PROPAGATION FROM SEED

1 Fill a small pot with compost (soil mix) and press down until it is firm.

2 Scatter the seed on the surface, giving an even distribution.

3 Cover with a fine gravel. Soak well and place in a bright but shady position where it is warm.

there will be a variety of sizes. Larger seedlings, up to thumb size, can be potted individually; smaller ones will grow much better if replanted in rows in a seed tray. They should be spaced about twice as far apart as their diameter, to allow for growth. Normal seed trays are quite shallow and need to be completely filled with compost (soil mix), so that there is enough compost (soil mix) and moisture to ensure a good growth rate. Seedlings should be watered regularly when they are dry, and the addition of a cactus fertilizer during the growing period will speed up the growth rate.

PRICKING OUT

Gently lift out the seedlings, taking care to avoid root damage. Sort by size.

POTTING UP

Pot up the larger seedlings into small individual pots. Replant small ones in rows in a seed tray and allow to grow on.

4 After germination, the plants make little growth for the first few months while they develop their root system.

5 Seedlings should be left alone for as long as possible before transplanting. These two year old seedlings are now ready to transplant. Notice the variation in size, which is quite normal.

Grafting

Some cacti are difficult to grow; others are slow-growing, making them difficult to propagate. Grafting is a way of making propagation easier and speeding up the growing process.

Grafting is the process of uniting the growing point of one cactus with the roots of another. In theory, all cacti are compatible and could be grafted. Normally, for grafting, the stock used is something that is quick-growing and will survive normal growing conditions easily. The tall-growing *Echinopsis* (the old genus *Trichocereus*) are an ideal choice.

Myrtillocactus and *Hylocereus* are suitable in very warm climates.

Grafting is achieved, very simply, by cutting the top from one plant (the stock) and the base from the piece you want to graft (the scion), and joining the two remaining pieces. It normally takes about two weeks for the stock and scion to unite.

Grafting is best carried out from late spring until mid-summer, when the weather is bright and the atmosphere dry, so that the exposed cut surfaces will dry quickly. Best results are achieved when both the stock and scion are healthy and growing well. After a little practice,

using both stock and scion that are growing well, you should achieve a success rate of over 90 per cent. If the grafting is being used to save a plant that appears to have started to die, however, the success rate is likely to be closer to 30 per cent. It is a useful technique, worth practising.

Flat grafting

This is the easiest method of grafting, with both the stock and scion cut at right angles to their length. The scion is easier to graft when its diameter is greater than its height. (If the scion is very slender, see below.) Collectors

SPLIT OR WEDGE GRAFTING

1 Take a length of something like the cylindrical *Selenicereus* up to about 90cm (3ft) tall. Cut horizontally across the top about 2.5cm (1in) below the growing point. With a sharp knife, cut vertically about 1cm (½in) down through the centre of the stock.

2 Take your slender scion, such as a Christmas cactus cutting, and carefully, with a sharp knife, remove the skin from the bottom 2cm (¾in) of the stem, leaving it slightly wedge shaped. Trim the end of the stem square and insert it into the slit in the stock.

3 Push a cactus spine right through the stock, to hold it in place, and either bind it with raffia or hold in position with a clothes peg (pin). The union should have been formed in about two weeks. A very tall, heavy stock will need to be supported on a cane or stick.

prefer a short stock, about 5cm (2in), so that, as the scion grows, the stock becomes invisible. If the scion is one of the brightly coloured, chlorophyll-less sports, however, a taller stock is needed, so that it can make enough food for both stock and scion.

Oblique grafting

Where the scion is very slender, cutting at an oblique angle will make a larger cut surface. This can either be placed at an angle on a flat stock and treated as a flat graft or, if the stock is also slender, it too can be cut obliquely. The more slender desert species, such as some *Echinocereus, Echinopsis* and *Peniocereus,* are probably best on a flat stock. The more slender epiphytic cacti, such as *Rhipsalis* and *Aporocactus,* are best grafted obliquely on to a slender stock like *Selenicereus.* Place the two cut surfaces together and use a cactus spine to pin them together. Bind with raffia, or hold in place with a clothes peg (pin) with a weakened spring.

Split or wedge grafting

The third method of grafting is a split or wedge graft. This method is useful for making taller epiphytes.

FLAT GRAFTING

1 Take a stock plant up to about 15cm (6in) tall and cut across the stem with a sharp knife, leaving about 5cm (2in) above the compost (soil mix) for a graft. On stocks with a hard skin, chamfer the edges.

3 Firmly push the scion on to the top of the stock so that their central core tissues touch. Rotate the scion to remove any trapped air bubbles.

2 Cut the base from the scion using a small knife or scalpel. Bevel 5mm (¼in) of skin from around the cut edge of the scion. Discard the base.

4 Secure in place with two rubber bands, placed at right angles over the scion; tight enough to exert a gentle pressure. Place the graft in a warm, bright position. After two weeks, remove the rubber bands and gently push sideways on the scion. Repeat the operation if it has not united.

Pests and diseases

Cacti are not particularly liable to pests and diseases, given reasonable cultivation. Most of the diseases that cacti suffer from are caused by being too wet and/or too cold. Check the label on insecticides and fungicides to see that they are suitable for application on cacti.

Mealy bug

How to identify: This is, perhaps, the worst pest to attack cacti. There are many different types of this pest, often associated with different types of host plant. Most of those types found on indoor plants seem to enjoy cactus as a host plant. It is like a small, white woodlouse with a very waxy coating. The nests, rather than the bug itself, are more often first noticed. The nests are like little blobs of cotton wool. When crushed, the small mealy bug is bright red and is the source of the dye cochineal.

Cause: Most pests are introduced from other infected plants.

Control: The best cure is first to remove by hand all traces of mealy bug by using a cotton swab dipped in denatured alcohol. In extreme infestation, treat the plant with a good systemic insecticide, one which is absorbed by the plant and poisons its sap. When the pests feed, they are killed. The addition of a little soap or wetting agent to a contact spray will help the spray penetrate the waxy coats of the plant.

Prevention: Check new additions carefully before introducing them to an established cacti collection. If desired, isolate new plants for a couple of weeks and monitor or treat with insecticide as a precaution.

Red spider mite

How to identify: This minute insect is more brown than red and is about the size of finely ground white pepper. It is hardly visible to the naked eye, and the first signs are usually a very fine but dense web, or the growing point of the plant turning brown, which gradually spreads down the plant body. Particularly noticeable on soft-skinned plants, such as *Rebutia*.

Cause: As with mealy bug, plants are most likely to become infected from contact with other plants.

Control: Regular spraying with miticide will control it.

Prevention: Monitor new plants before introducing them to the collection.

Basal and top rot

How to identify: Rotting from the base is usually an indication that plants have been over-watered. Young plants, particularly seedlings, are prone to damping off if too wet.

Cause: Rotting normally occurs in cool conditions but can also happen during very hot weather, when the plants may also go dormant, to conserve moisture. Top rotting is usually a sign of cold damage caused by exposure to frosts. Sometimes, tender new growth can scorch if the plants are moved from a shady position into full sun.

Control: Treating with a copper-based fungicide, such as Cheshunt compound, will control or prevent this problem. The rotting parts of larger plants should be cut out as soon as possible, with a sharp knife, and discarded. The tissue should be cut back so that there is no sign of discoloration or the rot will probably continue through the plant. The cut surfaces can either be left exposed to the air, if warm and dry, or treated with green sulphur.

Prevention: The use of a moisture gauge is the only accurate guide to the moisture content of the compost. In most cases, correcting the growing conditions will prevent most of these problems. Plants grown in a well drained compost (soil mix) and that are healthy and well fed are much more able to overcome minor adversities such as slight frost or harsh sunlight.

Etiolation

How to identify: A sudden change in the diameter of a plant and a generally stretched appearance.

Cause: This is usually due to lack of light but can also be caused by starvation.

Control: The problem can be corrected by placing the plant in a much brighter environment, although the constrictions will probably remain a permanent feature.

Prevention: Monitor the exposure to sunshine a plant receives, taking care not to scorch young plants.

■ ABOVE
Basal rot

■ OPPOSITE ABOVE LEFT
Cactus treated with green sulphur.

■ OPPOSITE LEFT
Mealy bug

■ OPPOSITE RIGHT
Red spider mite

■ THIS PAGE, FAR LEFT
Damping off

■ THIS PAGE, LEFT
Etiolated cactus

Calendar

Early spring

Repot any plants that have outgrown their containers and any that have not been touched for a long time. Wait at least a week after repotting before giving any water.

On warm, bright, sunny days, encourage the plants back into growth by the occasional light watering or spray. Sow seeds in a heated propagator.

Mid to late spring

As the weather improves, water occasionally until active new growth can be seen. As soon as the plants are growing again, commence regular waterings and feed about once per week. Allow the compost (soil mix) to dry out before watering again. Sow seeds on a windowsill or greenhouse without a propagator. Take cuttings and allow to callus. Now is a good time to start grafting.

Early to mid-summer

Remove germinated seedlings from the propagator to harden off and make room to sow some more. Pot calloused cuttings into a gritty compost (soil mix). Keep an eye out for pests and diseases and treat accordingly. Remember to water and feed your plants when they are dry. Slightly ease off watering the more mature desert plants, as many will become almost dormant in the height of summer. Keep epiphytes and seedlings shaded from the full sun, as they are prone to scorching.

Late summer

Begin to ease off watering and stop feeding, to give the new growth a chance to ripen before winter. As the days become shorter, and the nights colder, pots take very much longer to dry out. Treat all plants with an insecticide, so that they are pest-free for the winter. Stop grafting.

Parodia horstii – this produces striking summer displays of orange-red flowers.

Echinopsis huasha – red or gold funnel-shaped flowers appear in summer.

Early winter

Put the plants to rest until the spring. Gradually stop watering completely. Check heaters, and make sure that they work and are ready when needed. Examine the plants regularly for any disease, so that problems can be sorted out before they take a hold. Ventilate on warm, bright, sunny days. Start ordering seeds.

The longer winter nights are a good opportunity to read books, look at pictures and generally learn as much as possible about both the plants you are already growing and those you would like to grow. Seed lists are generally produced about this time of year, so plan and order what you want to grow next year.

Other recommended cacti

Acanthocalycium violaceum

Copiapoa barquitensis

Epithelantha mieromeris

Escobaria roseana

In recent years, there has been a major revision of the cactus plant family, reducing the number of valid species from over 6,000 to a little over 2,000. Many of these species are quite variable, so some of the old names have been retained as 'forms' to aid identification for the cactus collector, rather than for any botanical purpose.

Many of the popular genera have been reclassified and this list covers all the major, currently accepted genera, apart from those already mentioned in the Plant Catalogue. The list at the end of this section provides you with a quick update on some further new classifications for some of the rarer species.

Acanthocalycium Small-growing, globular to short, cylindrical plants, flowering from the crown in early summer. Easily grown.

Minimum temperature 5°C (42°F).

Ariocarpus 'Living Rock'. Very slow-growing and difficult. Plants grow flat to the ground. The angular tubercles are very pronounced and grey in colour. A little calcium (chalk) added to the soil will improve the root system.

Armatocereus Tall, tree-like, columnar cactus.

Arrojadoa Small, slender-stemmed plants. Minimum temperature 11°C (52°F). Flowers are small, tubular and very waxy. Requires warm conditions.

Arthrocereus Small-growing, often tuberous-rooted, difficult cactus.

Austrocactus Finger-like stems, fiercely spined. Difficult.

Aztekium Small, very slow-growing, disc-like plants. Difficult.

Blossfeldia The smallest growing cactus. Plants are button-like and slow-growing. Best grown grafted.

Carnegiea The giant Saguaro, often seen in Western films. Slow-growing in cultivation.

Coleocephalocereus Difficult. Minimum temperature 15°C (60°F). Plants produce wool down one side from the crown of mature plants, from which the flowers arise.

Copiapoa A very slow-growing group of globular cacti, from the coast of Chile.

Corryocactus Bush-like plant, with sharp spines and slender stems, initially erect, later arching to make big clumps.

Discocactus Small-growing, disc-like or globular plants, producing large, white, scented flowers at night in summer from the woolly crown. Difficult. Minimum temperature 15°C (60°F).

Disocactus A group of epiphytic cactus, with strap-like, flattened stems. Flowers are mostly small and funnel shaped. Minimum temperature 10°C (50°F).

Echinomastus Small, slow-growing, globular and very difficult plants.

Echinopsis oxygona With its globular shape and large, often scented, trumpet-shaped flowers produced at night, it is very popular. Minimum temperature 1°C (34°F).

Epithelantha Small, clumping plants, densely covered in very short, white or whitish spines. Not very easy, slow growing on their own roots, but grow well if grafted.

Escobaria Small-growing and small-flowering plants, usually densely spined. Moderately difficult. Minimum temperature 6°C (43°F).

Eulychnia South American columnar cactus.

Gymnocalycium quehlianum

Hatiora salicorniodes

Mammillaria candida

Mammillaria geminispina

Ferocactus pilosus Better known as *F. stainesii,* this plant has straight, bright red spines. Easy to grow. Needs to be about 25cm (10in) tall to flower. Minimum temperature 6°C (43°F).
Frailea Very small, globular to short, columnar plants. Plants often go from buds to seed pods without the flowers opening. When the weather conditions are right for the buds to open, the yellow flowers are usually larger than the plant. Not difficult but not very drought-resistant.
Gymnocactus Now *Turbinicarpus* or *Escobaria.*
Gymnocalycium quehlianum This disc-like species has a blue-grey or brownish body, always wider than tall. Flowers are produced from plants about 5cm (2in) in diameter.

Gymnocalycium saglionis One of the larger-growing, globular species, with attractive, curved, reddish spines, reaching up to 45cm (1½ft) diameter. The flowers are short and compact. Minimum temperature 6°C (43°F).
Haageocereus South American columnar cactus, 90cm–2m (3–6ft) tall, clumping. Usually densely covered in golden to brown spines.
Harrisia Tall-growing with slender, clambering stems. Purplish green sepals fringe a deep flowercup. Produces large white flowers at night. Easy.
Hatiora Reclassification has meant that this species now contains the Easter cactus and drunkard's dream. Small, bush-like epiphytic cactus, with short-jointed, flattened to cylindrical or angular, stems.

Heliocereus Epiphytic plants, with slender, creeping or pendant, angular stems. Flowers large and showy red or white. Minimum temperature 10°C (50°F).
Hylocereus Epiphyte. Slender, climbing stems producing large white flowers at night in summer. Minimum temperature 10–15°C (50–60°F).
Lepismium A group of pendant, slender-stemmed, epiphytic cactus, branching laterally to make large clumps. Stems sometimes cylindrical but often flat or triangular. Flowers small, white, cream pink or orange. Often confused with *Rhipsalis,* which branch in whorls from the tips of the stems.
Lophophora Small, slow-growing, almost spineless,

blue, globular bodies. Some plants in the wild produce an hallucinogen but this does not usually happen in cultivation. Because of its misuse, however, it is illegal in many countries.
Maihuenia Small, clumping, very slender-stemmed plants, related to the *Opuntia.* Semi-hardy and seems to grow better in cooler conditions in summer. Can be grown in a well-drained rockery but not very freely available.
Mammillaria candida The globular green body of this species is usually so densely covered in short white spines that it is not visible. Slow-growing, dislikes over-watering.
Mammillaria geminispina The arching, long, white, central spines and shorter

Mammillaria plumosa

Mammillaria zeilmanniana

Oraya neoperuviana

Parodia microsperma

radial ones give this plant a distinctive appearance. The shy, small pink flowers are produced in spring.
Mammillaria plumosa This cauliflower-like plant is densely covered in white spines. Difficult to grow; it flowers in mid-winter.
Mammillaria zeilmanniana One of the most popular commercial cacti, it is almost extinct in the wild. The small, dark purple-tinged bodies are densely covered in short, hooked spines.
Melocactus These globular plants, when mature, produce a woolly crown called a cephalium. With age, this grows taller, regularly producing small red to pink flowers in the summer afternoon sun, followed by large, sausage-shaped, red

fruits. These plants are difficult and require a minimum temperature of about 18°C (65°F) to do well.
Micranthocereus A small group of short, slender, cylindrical plants, clumping with age. Flowers are small and semi-tubular. Difficult. Minimum temperature 15°C (60°F).
Myrtillocactus Bush-forming, columnar cacti. Minimum temperature 12°C (54°F).
Neobuxbaumia Columnar cactus. Minimum temperature 11°C (52°F).
Neolloydia Includes *N. conuidea* and *N. matehualensis*, two species of small-growing, spiny, globular plants, clumping with age. Bright violet flowers in spring, from the crown of the plant. Difficult.

Oroya Small group of globular to disc-like plants, with small, orange-red to yellow flowers, produced in a ring around the crown of the plant in spring.
Parodia horstii Columnar with age, reaching 90cm (3ft) tall. Flowers in summer and autumn. Minimum temperature 6°C (43°F).
Parodia microsperma Difficult; dislikes both over-watering and prolonged dryness. Minimum temperature 6°C (43°F).
Pediocactus Slow-growing, globular cacti. Very difficult.
Pelecyphora Very slow-growing, small, globular cactus. Best grafted.
Peniocereus Slender-stemmed, often stick-like, many with large underground tubers, like a dahlia.

Pereskia Probably the most primitive cactus. Large-growing, bush-like or clambering, and one of the few cacti to put out leaves, often also producing abundant flowers. Many are very rapid growing and easy to cultivate but are too large for small greenhouses.
Pilosocereus Tall columnar cactus, often blue-skinned, making a woolly crown on mature flowering stems.
Pterocactus Small, tuberous-rooted plants, related to the *Opuntias*. Most make slender, prostrate, chocolate-coloured stems, which are brittle and easily broken or knocked off.
*Rebutia famatinensis (*Syn. *reicheocactus pseudoreichianus)* Firm, brown-coloured body; comparatively slow-growing.

Rebutia steinbachii f. *bicolor*

Rebutia famatinensis

Rebutia wessneriana

Turbinicarpus

Rebutia steinbachii f. *bicolor*
(**Syn.** *sulcorebutia bicolor*)
This robust species has sharp
black spines and variable
flower colours. One of the
easier *Sulcorebutias* to grow.
Rebutia wessneriana f.
krainziana Attractive short-
spined globular cacti with
attractive large red flowers.
Minimum temperature
5°C (42°F).
Rhipsalis (see also *Lepismium*)
A group of slender, pendant
or creeping stemmed,
epiphytic cacti. Stems can be
very slender, cylindrical to
angular or flat. Small, cream
to pink flowers are produced
on most species in
winter/spring, followed by
small, berry-like fruit. Now
separated from *Lepismium*
(which branch from the sides
of the stems), by the whorls of
new stems produced from the
tips of the old stems.
Schlumbergera Christmas- or
winter-flowering cactus.

Small, erect or pendant
bushes, producing their
flowers during winter. Make
good houseplants.
Sclerocactus An extremely
difficult group of small-
growing plants. Require low
night temperatures.
Stenocereus Tall-growing,
columnar cactus.
Strombocactus Small, slow-
growing and difficult.
Turbinicarpus Very small,
slow-growing plants,
flowering when quite young
from the crown. Not easy and
require a very free-draining
compost (soil mix).
Uebelmannia A small group
of globular to short,
cylindrical plants. Difficult.
Minimum temperature 11°C
(52°F).
Weberbauerocereus Tall
columnar cacti, often branching to make tree-like shapes.
Weberocereus A group of
slender-stemmed, creeping or
climbing, epiphytic cacti.

Further checklist of new and former cacti classifications

Aylostera see *Rebutia*
Bolivicereus see *Cleistocactus*
Borzicactus see *Cleistocactus*
  and Matucana
Chamaecereus see *Echinopsis*
  chamaecereus
Cryptocereus see *Selenicereus*
  imitans
Deamia see *Selenicereus*
  testudo
Dolicothele see *Mammillaria*
Echinofossulocactus see
  Stenocactus
Erdisia see *Corryocactus*
Eriocactus see *Parodia*
Eriocereus see *Harrisia*
Helianthocereus see
  Echinopsis
Hildewinteria see
  Cleistocactus winteri
Horridocactus see *Eriosyce*
Islaya see *Eriosyce islayensis*
Lemairocereus see *Stenocereus*
Lobivia see *Echinopsis*
Loxanthocereus see
  Cleistocactus

Malacocarpus see *Parodia*
Monvillea see *Cereus*
Neochilenia see *Eriosyce*
Neoporteria see *Eriosyce*
Nopalea see *Opuntia*
Nopalxochia see *Disocactus*
Notocactus see *Parodia*
Pfeiffera see *Lepismium*
Phyllocactus see *Epiphyllum*
Pseudolobivia see *Echinopsis*
Pyrrhocactus see *Eriosyce*
Rhipsalidopsis see *Hatiora*
Setiechinopsis see *Echinopsis*
Soehrensia see *Echinopsis*
Sulcorebutia see *Rebutia*
Tephrocactus see *Opuntia*
Toumeya see *Pediocactus,*
  Turbinicarpus and
  Sclerocactus
Trichocereus see *Echinopsis*
Weingartia see *Rebutia*
Wigginsia see *Parodia*
Wilcoxia see *Echinocereus*
Wittea see *Disocactus*
  amazonicus
Zygocactus see *Schlumbergera*

Index

Echinocereus viridiflorus

Echinopsis aurea

Rebutia arenacea

ACKNOWLEDGEMENTS
The publishers would like to thank the following people for their help in the production of this book: Holly Gate Cactus Nursery, West Sussex and Mr. and Mrs. Darbon, Oxford. All pictures were taken by Peter Anderson with the exception of the following by Juliette Wade: p14bl, p15, p16, p49tr and Stephanie Donaldson: p14tr.